I0104074

Transparent and Inclusive Stakeholder Participation through Public Councils in Kazakhstan

OECD

BETTER POLICIES FOR BETTER LIVES

This work is published under the responsibility of the Secretary-General of the OECD. The opinions expressed and arguments employed herein do not necessarily reflect the official views of OECD member countries.

This document, as well as any data and map included herein, are without prejudice to the status of or sovereignty over any territory, to the delimitation of international frontiers and boundaries and to the name of any territory, city or area.

Please cite this publication as:

OECD (2020), *Transparent and Inclusive Stakeholder Participation through Public Councils in Kazakhstan*, OECD Public Governance Reviews, OECD Publishing, Paris, *https://doi.org/10.1787/d21f1e98-en*.

ISBN 978-92-64-78514-4 (print)
ISBN 978-92-64-44257-3 (pdf)

OECD Public Governance Reviews
ISSN 2219-0406 (print)
ISSN 2219-0414 (online)

Foreword

Open government promotes the principles of transparency, integrity, accountability and stakeholder participation in support of democracy and inclusive growth. Countries around the world increasingly acknowledge that open government can improve government efficiency and effectiveness, while bringing the administration and its officials closer to citizens.

Kazakhstan has been working to make its government more open, and to engage citizens and civil society in the policy making process. To this end, it created public councils made up of civil society representatives and public officials.

Following the 2017 OECD Review on Open Government in Kazakhstan, OECD has been working with the Government of the Republic of Kazakhstan to support the implementation of the Review's recommendations. The Review highlighted the need for more clarity in the functions that the public councils are expected to perform, to ensure their transparency and increase their effectiveness.

This report focuses on improving the practices of public councils as mechanisms for stakeholder participation in Kazakhstan, drawing on the 2017 Recommendation of the Council of the OECD on Open Government. Specifically, it encourages the Kazakhstan authorities to develop guidelines that will cover all procedures pertaining to the functioning of public councils to reduce the level of discretion of each entity. It also provides recommendations on the methodologies required for public consultation in the regulatory process. Kazakhstan could also strengthen mechanisms for active and meaningful civil society participation in the assessment of local executive bodies' performance, including of their effectiveness, responsiveness, and openness. Such mechanisms could include publishing the results of the assessments of their activities, and on the actions to be taken based on the results of these assessments.

To date, Kazakhstan authorities have taken steps to implement these recommendations, including passing two key laws on access to information and on the creation of public councils as instruments of government collaboration with civil society. In addition, the Ministry of Social Development has revised the model on which councils are created.

The present report was produced under the OECD Kazakhstan Country Programme, which seeks to facilitate the reforms in the areas of organisation and management of the public sector, decentralisation, openness and transparency, and gender-sensitive decision-making processes, in view of promoting Kazakhstan's adherence to OECD instruments and use of good practices from OECD members.

The information, data, and evidence used to develop the recommendations were collected through desk research conducted by the OECD Secretariat, a fact-finding mission to Astana and the Western Kazakhstan region, and a qualitative survey disseminated to regional and municipal public councils.

Acknowledgements

This report was drafted by Hille Hinsberg, Policy Analyst of the OECD Open Government Unit, as part of the Kazakhstan Country programme. It was drafted under the supervision of Alessandro Bellantoni, Head of the Open Government Unit and Martin Forst, Head of the Governance Reviews and Partnerships Division of the OECD Public Governance Directorate. Amelia Godber provided editorial support.

The OECD thanks the peer reviewers who participated in the fact-finding mission to Astana and Uralsk and shared their experience at a workshop held in Astana to reflect on the preliminary findings and recommendations of this report: Dmytro Khutkyy, Manager, E-Democracy Group of Ukraine, Thomas Rogé, Head of the Youth Policy Department in the City of Paris, France, and Iain Murray, policy officer of the Public Service Reform and Community Planning Department of the Scottish Government, United Kingdom.

The report team wishes to acknowledge the significant contribution made by their interlocutors in the Republic of Kazakhstan: the Ministry of Information and Communication and in particular: Vice-Minister of Information and Communications of the Republic of Kazakhstan Nurgul Mauberlinova, Vice-Minister of Information and Communications of the Republic of Kazakhstan Dinara Sheglova, Deputy Head of Policy Department Bekzat Rakhimov and Chief Policy Expert on Access to Information Elmira Nurkisheva; in the Ministry of Social Development (formerly Ministry for Religious Affairs and Civil Society), in particular: Vice Chairman of the Committee for Civil Society Affairs Gulbara Sultanova, and Senior Expert for Civil Society Affairs Kairat Baimuldinov.

Special thanks to Gabidulla Ospankulov, Deputy Akim of the West Kazakhstan region and staff at the Uralsk Oblast Akimat for arranging the fact-finding visit to the West Kazakhstan region.

Special thanks to all interlocutors during the fact-finding mission, including Marat Kogamov, Chairman of the Public Council at the Ministry of Internal Affairs of the Republic of Kazakhstan, and Altynai Kobejeva, Secretary of the Public Council of the city of Almaty.

Valuable information was provided by Askar Kushkunbayev and Anton Artemyev from the Soros Foundation Kazakhstan.

The authors would like to thank Joao Vasconselos, Policy Analyst from the OECD Digital Government Unit for his contribution to the workshop in Astana on citizen-driven policy-making and public service delivery by digital tools.

Table of Contents

Tables

Figures

Boxes

Follow OECD Publications on:

http://twitter.com/OECD_Pubs

http://www.facebook.com/OECDPublications

http://www.linkedin.com/groups/OECD-Publications-4645871

http://www.youtube.com/oecdilibrary

OECD
Alerts http://www.oecd.org/oecddirect/

Executive summary

Kazakhstan is taking steps towards greater openness, is striving to ensure the transparency of government-held information and data by publishing official decisions and improving access to public services, including through digital channels. Yet, like many other countries around the world, it faces complex challenges on the path towards open government, which the OECD defines as "a culture of governance that promotes the principles of transparency, integrity, accountability and stakeholder participation in support of democracy and inclusive growth."

Enabling policy and legal framework for open government

The government of Kazakhstan has shown a strong interest in enhancing transparency, accountability and participation in the policy-making cycle in order to strengthen public trust in government and improve the quality of public services. As part of the Kazakhstan 2050 Strategy, the government has developed five institutional reforms to help reinforce the capacity of the state to fulfil its objective of being among the 30 most-developed countries in the world by 2050. One of these five institutional reforms is "Transparency and Accountability of the State", which underlines the administration's commitment to open government reforms.

Kazakhstan has already made significant achievements in this field, including the approval of an access to information (ATI) law and the creation of public councils as the institutions dedicated to enable citizen participation. Still, further steps could be taken to strengthen the participation of stakeholders in policy-making and ensure the incorporation of open government principles in Kazakhstan's governance culture.

Among the priorities yet to be addressed by the administration is the need to establish a single definition of open government that is fully recognised and acknowledged by the whole public sector, and communicated to and accepted by all stakeholders. According to OECD good practices, this definition, together with the development of a structured and holistic open government strategy, are crucial for broadening the scope and impact of Kazakhstan's open government agenda.

The definition and strategy would help to ensure a level playing field for non-governmental actors, including hybrid bodies (i.e. combinations of public and independent institutions) such as public councils and business chambers, which act as regular advisory partners to the administration.

Public council as a mechanism for stakeholder participation

Kazakhstan has institutionalised stakeholder participation in the policy cycle through the creation of public councils, in which two-third of the seats are assigned to civil society and one-third to public officials. Suggestions by the public councils are advisory in nature, but their consideration is obligatory for all relevant public institutions, which are required to provide a response. Accordingly, through this provision public councils play an important role whenever public officials are tasked to produce policy proposals, evaluate the performance of public institutions, and make suggestions to improve services.

The main positive features of public councils can be summarised as follows:

- The law upon which the councils were established gives clear instruction to both officials and stakeholders on the mandate and functions of councils;
- Councils are proving effective in improving the transparency of the decision-making process by disseminating relevant information about the activities of the public institution they are attached to.
- Councils act as a unique platform in the country for involving civil society stakeholders in the policy-making cycle as well as in the evaluation of public services.
- Councils are permanent institutions. Hence, even if members rotate, the format of a permanent council enables gradual accumulation of expertise and improves the culture of governance.

Recommendations to improve the governance of public councils

If the government seeks to empower councils to effectively give voice to citizens' concerns and perform their control functions, as mandated by the law, the councils' governance should be further improved by: including a greater diversity of citizen groups, conducting operations in a more transparent manner, and to better facilitate the stakeholders' expertise and proposals as valuable input to decisions taken by public institutions. Key recommendations focus on applying standard requirements for establishing and managing councils. In particular:

- The transparency of councils as a mechanism for stakeholder participation could be improved by disclosing more information on their composition, including publishing criteria for nominating their members.
- Councils' transparency needs to be upheld in an ongoing manner by regularly disseminating information about the councils' work and its impact.
- Councils should be granted greater financial autonomy.
- The public institution that establishes a public council, be it a municipality or a ministry, should consider covering the costs related to procuring external expertise, such as legal advisory services, carrying out site visits to monitor public services, or conducting other activities to ensure that councils carry out their functions according to the criteria set by the law.

Recommendations to improve the functions of public councils as mandated by law

Among the functions of the public councils foreseen by the law is to provide expert opinions on draft regulations from the perspective of civil society. However, the public consultation process currently lacks explicit calls for comments, clear timelines, and guidance on how to report on the use of the feedback received. Accordingly:

- Clearer guidelines on how to conduct public consultation processes would benefit councils, and in general all stakeholders, and would encourage their engagement in providing input into policy-making. In order to ensure that the consultation process is as inclusive and representative as possible, councils need to engage with all relevant stakeholders.

- Specific training on how to carry out inclusive consultations should be made available for civil servants and public councils' members.

It is recommended to pay particular attention to closing the feedback loop by providing stakeholders with detailed feedback on the use of their comments and by following up on the implementation of the proposals made by public councils. Only by creating a responsive dialogue with the authorities can public councils serve their purpose of improving the accountability of public institutions in Kazakhstan.

Chapter 1. Stakeholder participation as a pillar of Open Government

This chapter defines and explains OECD principles and practices related to stakeholder participation as a pillar of Open Government, providing a framework of enablers for systematic integration of participation into policy making.

Levels of participation

Participation can be understood as the interaction, either formal or informal, between government, citizens, and other stakeholders, including civil society organisations (CSOs), academia, and the private sector, which is used to inform a specific policy outcome in a manner that ensures well-informed decision making and avoids policy capture (OECD, 2016a).

The OECD Recommendation on Open Government defines stakeholder participation as "all the ways in which stakeholders can be involved in the policy cycle and in service design and delivery" (OECD, 2017a).

The Recommendation, alongside other standard-setting legal instruments of the OECD (2015a, 2015b) conveys the belief that:

- Stakeholder participation is an essential part of an inclusive and transparent policy-making process.
- The enabling legal, policy and institutional frameworks for stakeholder participation must be connected and coordinated with other elements of open government, such as ensuring access to information, integrity of public service, and responsiveness of public sector institutions.
- Stakeholder participation is a structured approach to interact with stakeholders at any moment of the policy cycle about any policy decisions and about public service design and delivery.

Open government implies three different but complementary and increasing levels of citizen-government relationships (Figure 1.1)

Information is a one-way relationship in which governments produce and deliver information to be used by citizens. It covers both "passive" access to information upon citizen demand and "active" measures by government to disseminate information to citizens. Examples include access to public records, official gazettes and government websites. Access to information is part of the legal frameworks of most countries today. It is an important precondition for citizens' abilities to enquire, scrutinise and contribute to decision making (Gavelin, Burall and Wilson, 2009) and a key building block of open government reforms.

Kazakhstan's Law on Access to Information sets standards for all public bodies for disclosing government information and ensuring the availability of public data. It also specifies the obligation to respond to citizens' requests for information. The law applies to bodies and institutions of the legislative, executive, and judicial branches of state power, as well as local administration. Any other state-affiliated institutions as well as quasi-state sectors are also subject to the law.

Public Councils follow the requirements to disclose information about their constitution, their activities and their results.

Access to information is a necessary, but on its own, insufficient precondition for effective citizen participation, as the provision of information does not automatically lead to participation. It is the attributes of the information disclosed, including its relevance to the concerns of stakeholders and its usability, that make the difference in the actual use of information for engagement and influencing policy decisions (OECD, 2016).

Figure 1.1. Levers of stakeholder participation

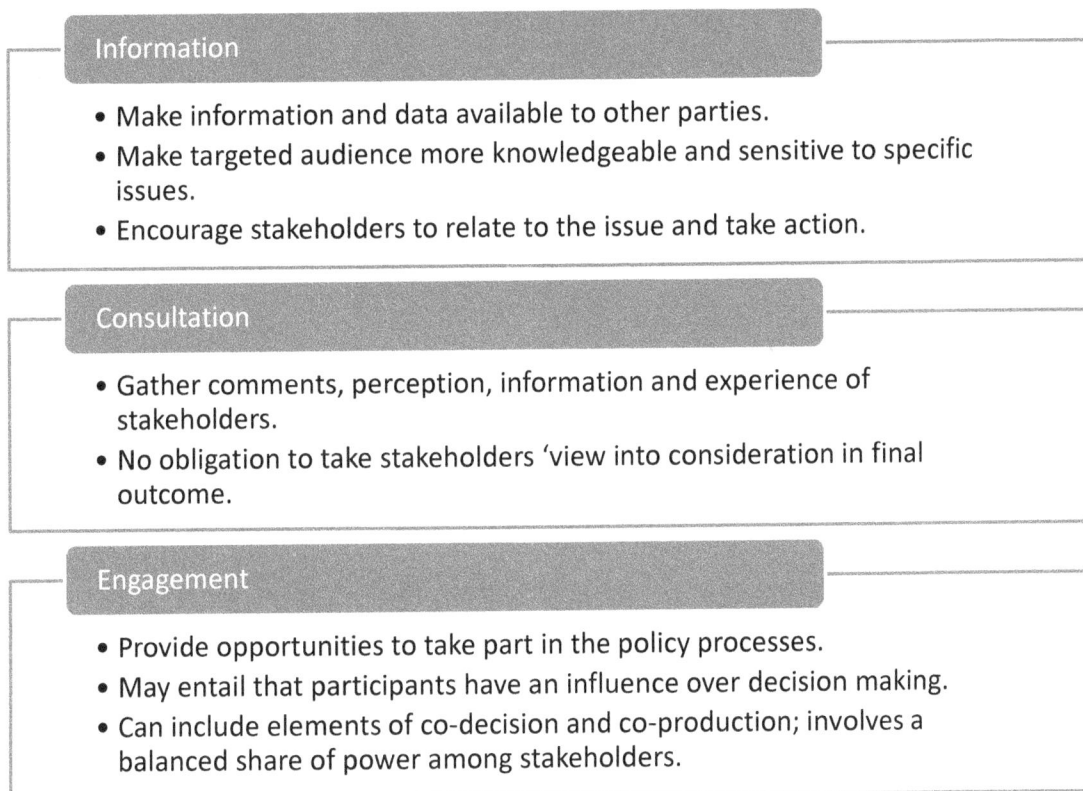

Information

- Make information and data available to other parties.
- Make targeted audience more knowledgeable and sensitive to specific issues.
- Encourage stakeholders to relate to the issue and take action.

Consultation

- Gather comments, perception, information and experience of stakeholders.
- No obligation to take stakeholders 'view into consideration in final outcome.

Engagement

- Provide opportunities to take part in the policy processes.
- May entail that participants have an influence over decision making.
- Can include elements of co-decision and co-production; involves a balanced share of power among stakeholders.

Source: OECD (2016), Open Government: The Global Context and the Way Forward, OECD Publishing, Paris,

Consultation is a two-way relationship in which citizens provide feedback to government (comments, perceptions, information, advice, experiences and ideas). It is based on the prior definition by government of the issues on which citizens' views are being sought that require provision of information. Governments define the issues for consultation, set the questions and manage the process, while citizens are invited to contribute their views and opinions. The process is often initiated by decision makers looking for insights and views from stakeholders involved or who will likely be affected by the outcomes (OECD, 2016).

Some 94% of OECD countries require public consultation on some or all primary laws (OECD, 2015).

In Kazakhstan, it is obligatory to consider the opinion of National Business Chamber Atameken on all regulatory acts that have a potential effect on business environment and entrepreneurial activities (Law on the National Business Association Atameken).

Public Councils are invited to provide their comments on regulatory acts, but these are recommendatory in nature (Law on Public Councils).

Engagement or active participation is a relationship based on a partnership between citizens and governments. Citizens actively engage in defining the process and content of policy-making. Like consultation, engagement is based on a two-way interaction. It acknowledges equal standing for citizens in setting the agenda, proposing policy options and shaping the policy dialogue, although the responsibility for the final decision or policy formulation rests with the government in many instances (OECD, 2016).

Engagement recognises the capacity of citizens to discuss and generate policy options in collaboration with the government. It requires governments to design their agendas with citizens and relies on governments' commitment that policy proposals generated jointly will have an impact on the policy cycle (Corella, 2011). At the same time, engagement requires citizens to accept their increased responsibility for policy making. Engagement practices need to provide sufficient time and flexibility to allow for the emergence of new ideas and proposals by citizens, as well as mechanisms for their integration into government policy-making processes.

Nowadays, countries are increasingly exploring methods of actively engaging citizens in creating policies and co-designing and co-delivering services.

> *In Kazakhstan, the activities of public councils in initiating and conducting public monitoring of services is a good example of citizen engagement in the evaluation and monitoring of government activities with the aim of improving service quality and user-centric delivery.*

> *The functions of public councils are described by Kazakh regulations as exercising "public control", which implies the objective of holding government institutions accountable for their performance. However, the councils do not and should not have a mandate for oversight over public institutions.*

This role is in the hands of elected representative bodies such as local councils (*Maslihat*), the Parliament, and independent oversight institutions, such as the Information Commission or auditing institutions. In general, control and oversight bodies or institutions are usually either independent from the entity that they are supposed to control or solely composed of members of that entity (e.g. an internal control unit). This is not the case with councils, as they are affiliated with public institutions, and public officials form 1/3 of their membership.

Therefore, the public councils are a participatory format, with some elements that support the accountability of institutions. Accountability is an interactive process that requires that those held accountable explain their decisions and actions, and that defines the external stakeholders' right and ability to inquire about those actions (Fox, 2014).

Throughout this report, the analysis and recommendations target the goal of ensuring that the councils can effectively perform their role of promoting citizen's active participation.

Enablers of citizen participation

Governments are responsible for encouraging citizens and stakeholder participation by creating an enabling environment and establishing appropriate legal, policy and institutional frameworks to help remove obstacles for the participation of everyone, and especially of those who are frequently excluded, for example youth, women or marginalised groups of society (OECD, 2017b).

The following analysis and recommendations are structured into four aspects that constitute the main enablers for stakeholders' participation (see Figure 1.2).

Figure 1.2. Enablers for participation

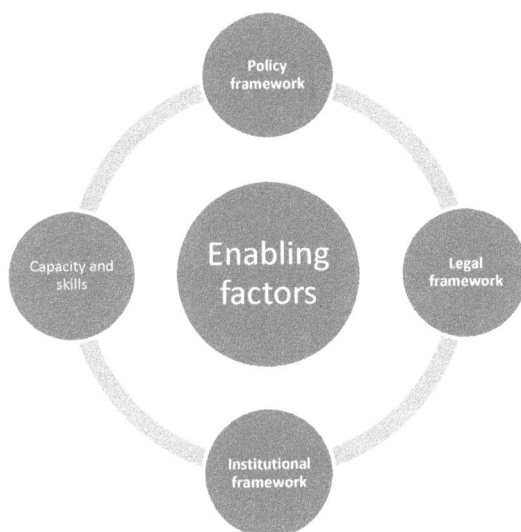

- **Policy framework**, including open government, anti-corruption, or digital government strategies
- **Legal framework**, including regulations and administrative procedures;
- **Institutional framework,** including financial and human resources, and related institutions to support participation practice;
- **Capacity, i.e. the awareness, motivation and skills** of policy-makers such as elected officials and civil servants to conduct participatory processes.

To create a shift towards participatory culture in policy-making, best practices from OECD countries suggest adopting a holistic approach by addressing all the above-mentioned enabling factors. Focusing on one component only, e.g. by merely adopting regulation but not supporting its implementation by building capacities, does not enhance participation. Furthermore, political and cultural attitudes are also part of creating a favourable environment for effective participation.

References

Corella B. (2011), Citizen engagement to enhance accountability and prevent corruption in the provision of public services in OECD countries.

http://unpan1.un.org/intradoc/groups/public/documents/un-dpadm/unpan047621.pdf

Gavelin K., Burall S. Wilson R. (2009), Open Government: beyond static measures. Involve for the OECD.

Fox, J. (2014). Social Accountability: What Does the Evidence Really Say? Global Partnership for Social Accountability Working Paper. Washington, D.C.: The World Bank.

OECD (2017a), Recommendation of the Council on Open Government, OECD Publishing, Paris.

OECD (2017b), Towards an Open Government in Kazakhstan, OECD Public Governance Reviews, OECD Publishing, Paris.

OECD (2016), Open Government. The global context and the way forward, OECD Publishing, Paris.

OECD (2015a), Recommendation of the Council on Budgetary Governance", OECD Publishing, Paris.

OECD (2015b), Recommendation of the Council on Gender Equality in Public Life", OECD Publishing, Paris.

Law on the National Business Association Atameken, http://kazkenes.kz/laws

Law on Public Councils, as amended on July 11, 2017 http://kazkenes.kz/laws

Law on Legal Acts, https://legalacts.egov.kz/

State of the Nation Address by President of Kazakhstan Nursultan Nazarbayev. November 30, 2015, http://www.akorda.kz/en/addresses/state-of-the-nation-address-by-president-of-kazakhstan-nursultan-nazarbayev-november-30-2015

Chapter 2. Analysis of and recommendations on improving the participation functions of public councils

This chapter describes the current situation in Kazakhstan vis-à-vis the enabling factors of open government. All aspects are analysed according to information collected on the current practices of public councils in implementing their functions described in the legislative and policy frameworks.

Policy and legal framework

Widely accepted principles of good governance include openness, transparency and accountability, as well as fairness and equity in the government's relationship with its citizens, including mechanisms for consultation and participation. Good governance also entails efficient and effective services; clear, transparent and enforced laws and regulations; consistency and coherence in policy formation; and respect for the rule of law and high standards of ethical behaviour. These principles represent the basis upon which open government is built (OECD, 2017b).

These principles can be put to practice by means of a policy framework that enables good governance implementation.

Policy framework. Open government as one of the 100 Concrete Steps to implement the Kazakhstan 2050 Strategy

To implement the Kazakhstan 2050 Strategy, the government of Kazakhstan has developed five institutional reforms that will help the country strengthen the state and help it achieve its goal of placing Kazakhstan among the 30 most advanced economies in the world by 2050, as expressed in the Kazakhstan 2050 Strategy. One of these five institutional reforms is transparency and accountability of the state.

Furthermore, these five institutional reforms are implemented by the 100 Concrete Steps announced by President Nursultan Nazarbayev in 2015. The following steps were established to support a more transparent and accountable state:

- Step 94: Introduction of "open government". Drafting law on access to information that will allow access to any information belonging to state agencies, except for highly confidential state documents and other information protected by the law.

- Step 95: Introduction of annual public statements by heads of state agencies on achieving key objectives and the publication of their reports on official websites. Introduction of annual reports on the performance of heads of national higher education institutions.

- Step 96: Ensuring online access to statistical data belonging to central state agencies. All budget, spending and consolidated financial reports, as well as the results of external assessments of the quality of state services will be published.

- Step 97: Empowering citizens to participate in the decision-making process by developing local governance. Giving more powers to the private sector and self-regulated organisations, especially for activities that are not typically performed by the state.

- Step 98: Independent budgets for local government will be introduced in rural areas (*Auyls*, villages and towns). Mechanisms will be put in place to allow citizens to participate in discussing the best ways to spend the budget.

- Step 99: Strengthening the role of public councils under state agencies and *Akims* (heads of a local government in Kazakhstan and Kyrgyzstan). These councils will discuss the implementation of strategic plans and regional development programmes, as well as budgets, reports, achieving stated objectives, draft legal acts concerning rights and freedoms of citizens, and draft programme documents. Legally establishing these public councils will enhance the transparency of state decision making.

In many OECD countries, open government themes are simultaneously part of countries' national strategies and the related sector policies. In addition, open government principles and practices can inform the ways in which the strategies, sectoral policies and implementation phases are designed and delivered. Accordingly, in 49% of OECD countries, there is a single national open government strategy, while in 51% there is no single national open government strategy, instead open government initiatives that are integrated into other sector initiatives, policies or strategies (OECD (2017b).

Box 2.1. An example of a national open government strategy

Netherlands

The central government of the Netherlands recently published its Open Government in Action (Open overheid in actie) Plan for 2016-17. The progressive policy document presents nine concrete commitments that touch on almost all of the elements of the OECD's definition of open government. The first three commitments call for better availability of government data to the public. Commitment 4 goes beyond the publishing of data and calls for disclosing reports of examinations, public procurement, subsidies and performance tests. Moreover, the Action Plan explicitly includes open decision-making at the local level (Commitment 6). As a central element for the successful implementation of the Action Plan, the plan lists the main ministries responsible for its implementation as well as the ministries in charge of assistance. Every commitment also entails tangible and concrete indicators on how to measure progress and possibly the successful implementation of the commitment by 2017.

Source: Based on the Netherlands' response to the "OECD Open Government Survey 2015".

As mentioned above, Kazakhstan has foreseen open government principles in its long-term strategy, Kazakhstan 2050. Moving towards a more transparent and open state is supported by Kazakhstan's participation in other initiatives promoting transparency, such as the Extractive Industries Transparency Initiative (EITI) and the Open Budget Index.

Kazakhstan's responses to the "OECD Open Government Survey" noted that Step 94 "Introduction of the open government" of the Plan of the Nation (i.e., the 100 Concrete Steps to implement the "Five Institutional Reforms") constitutes its national open government strategy. This step foresees the: "drafting of a law on access to information that will allow access to any information of state agencies except for highly confidential state documents and other information protected by the law." Yet, despite the importance of these legal commitments and the emphasis on transparency and accountability in the 100 Concrete Steps Plan of the Nation, there does not appear to be any comprehensive national strategy for open government. Indeed, the lack of a national strategy on open government was noted as one of the five challenges for the implementation of open government initiatives as part of the OECD Survey on Open Government Coordination. Therefore, to further support the implementation of the presidential agenda, it would be important for Kazakhstan to consider the development of a full-fledged open government strategy that includes principles, long-term outcomes, medium-term outputs and concrete initiatives to be carried out in collaboration with citizens, civil society organisations and the private sector (OECD, 2017b)

To develop its single and national open government strategy, Kazakhstan needs to take into account that such a strategy is intended to be a document that applies to the whole public sector and that highlights the **principles**, **policy objectives**, and **policy instruments or initiatives** of the county's open government reform agenda. Policy objectives correspond to the "ends" of the strategy and reflect the overall purpose or medium-term aim(s), which a strategy eventually seeks to achieve (OECD, 2016).

The objectives stated in the president's speech and in the main national policy objectives that the government of Kazakhstan intends to achieve by implementing an open government strategy are in line with those of most OECD countries:

- improve the transparency of the public sector

- improve the accountability of the public sector

- improve the efficiency of the public sector

- prevent and fight corruption

- increase citizens' trust in public institutions.

Furthermore, the open government strategy should also include policy instruments and initiatives, which are the "means" of a strategy – the actions used to carry it out – and the methods by which its objectives are to be achieved (OECD, 2016). All OECD countries are currently implementing, or have implemented, open government initiatives, with a focus on initiatives on digital government, open data and access to information.

This is in line with Kazakhstan's approach towards open government, as it has been mostly driven by an open data agenda. The Kazakhstan government set the development of e-government as a priority, being the first country in Central Asia to develop an e-government initiative (OECD (2017b).

Recently the Government of Kazakhstan has developed a more structured approach to the development of open government in the country. According to http://open.egov.kz, it includes four main components:

- *open legislation*

- *open data*

- *open dialogue*

- *open budgets*

However, even though these components are clearly stated as aspects of open government, without a more articulated document that describes which activities are going to be carried out, how they are going to be achieved, by when and who will be responsible for them, it is difficult to assess the strategy's potential effects on the government and society as a whole. For each of these components, Kazakhstan could develop a more extensive plan in cooperation with civil society and in line with the elements contained in the national open government strategy suggested above OECD (2017b).

The legal framework in Kazakhstan is largely in place for introducing regular stakeholder participation into the policy-making cycle (Table 2.1). Citizens can obtain information concerning political decisions which would be formulated into regulatory acts, and they are invited to express their opinion through channels for public consultation, giving feedback on draft documents.

Table 2.1. Regulatory framework to support stakeholder participation in policy-making

Regulatory aspect	In place?
Obligation to respond to citizens' requests for information.	Yes. Law on Access to Information sets standards for all public bodies for disclosing government information, ensuring availability of public information proactively, and the obligation to handle requests for information.
Obligation to publish draft legislation before its adoption	Yes. Normative acts have to be published on central public website Open Legislation
Obligation to conduct impact assessment on policy measures in normative acts or strategy documents	No. If any analytical assessment is conducted, it is not obligatory or customary to include the document in the file disclosed for public opinion.
Obligation to conduct formalized public consultation on legal acts	Yes. It is obligatory to consider the opinion of Atameken on all normative acts that have a potential effect on business environment and entrepreneurial activities. Public Councils are invited to provide comments on draft normative acts. The authorities are obliged to consider their proposals.
Obligation that proposals of laws that are presented to proceedings by local government, central government or parliament bodies need to be accompanied by a report on stakeholders' input.	No. The authorities are obliged to give feedback but there is no formal template, nor formally established status in the dossier of regulatory documents.

Source: Based on OECD (2014), Regulatory Policy in Kazakhstan: Towards Improved Implementation, OECD Publishing, Paris and relevant laws.

Law on Public Councils

The Law on Public Councils was adopted in December 2015. This instrument of public councils to support transparency and stakeholder participation is thus quite recent.

The purpose of this law is mainly to enhance the transparency of the process and content of lawmaking by providing requirements for the procedure of making draft legal acts public and accessible for public comments:

- "Ensure and increase the transparency with regard to public and stakeholders participation in policy and decision making processes of public bodies,
- Fulfilling the objectives of good, transparent and inclusive governance in the decision-making processes."

The creation of the public council was a priority for the government, as indicated in the 99th Step of the 100 Concrete Steps in State of the Nation Address by President of Kazakhstan Nursultan Nazarbayev, 2015:

> *"Strengthening the role of Public Councils under state institutions and Akims. They will discuss the implementation of strategic plans and regional development programs, as well as budgets, reports, achieving stated objectives, draft legal acts concerning rights and freedoms of citizens, and draft program documents. Legally establishing these public councils will enhance transparency of state decision-making."*

As noted in the OECD Review on Open Government in Kazakhstan (OECD, 2017b), public councils have been largely used by transition or developing countries, including in the former Soviet Union, sub-Saharan Africa, South Asia, and Latin America, as a mechanism for government to foster citizen cooperation.

In some OECD member countries, advisory councils are used also at the subnational level to support the local communities in their interaction with authorities.

Open Government is relevant for subnational governments. On the one hand, policies on transparency, engagement and accountability can strengthen the performance of subnational governments, ensuring that policies and services are responsive to local needs, thereby promoting trust in government. On the other hand, subnational governments "have a key role in implementing open government practices and initiatives as they are at the forefront of the state and many of the open government's recommendations and commitments have direct implications at the local level" (OECD, 2016).

Moreover, subnational authorities are the place where citizens and policies meet (OECD, 2016a). The proximity of citizens to the state spurs engagement, but also shapes citizens' perception of the government. The rise of the involvement of citizens in policy-making goes hand in hand "with the decentralisation efforts initiated by many countries from the seventies and consisted of transferring authority, responsibility, and resources from the national government to lower governmental levels to better respond to citizens' needs and demands" (OECD, 2016). Subnational governments remain a space for innovative and interactive forms of governance, including diverse formats for facilitating stakeholder participation in public policies and service design.

In Scotland for example, the councils are formed for each district council area. There are 32 Community Planning Partnerships (CPPs) across Scotland. The title refers to the method of collaborative community planning. Each CPP is responsible for developing and delivering a plan for its council area.

Community planning partnerships secure the participation of communities throughout the cycle of developing local priorities, including the design, development, delivery of development plans and their review, revision and reporting.

Community planning partnerships strive to report publicly to their communities in an accessible and comprehensible manner (Box 2.2).

Box 2.2. Scotland. Community Planning Partnerships

Community planning encourages local public sector bodies to work closely with people in communities to deliver the services they need most. The underlying principles are that designing public services with and for communities is better than expecting people and communities to fit into public services.

CPPs are formed by a diverse range of local authorities, including National Health Service boards and joint boards for integrating health and social care, Police Scotland, Scottish Fire and Rescue Service, Scottish Enterprise, Highlands and Islands Enterprise, regional colleges, regional transport partnerships, Skills Development Scotland and Scottish Natural Heritage.

The aims and principles of CPPs are described in the Community Empowerment Act of 2015, which provides a general framework. To achieve their goals and carry out the foreseen tasks, CPPs have a flexible organisation. The main principle is to make sure that everyone involved is clear about what they have agreed to do and who is responsible for which tasks.

It is stated in the Act and its guidance that participation of communities lies at the heart of community planning, and should be applied in the development, design and delivery of plans as well as in the review, revision and reporting. CPPs must report every year to their communities. They have to let their communities know what progress they have made in improving the lives of local people. Reports about progress, whether good or bad, should be easily available to the local community, so that communities can see and understand what has changed because of community planning. Reports should explain what the priorities are and show how things have improved or worsened.

The guidance to explain CPPs work states that "Community planning does not replace the activities that these public sector bodies do on their own as part of their everyday work. For example, local CPPs aren't responsible for fighting fires. But community planning partners and local communities could work together with the Fire and Rescue Service to prevent fires from happening in the first place. They might for instance work together to make sure they share information, understanding and sharing resources so that helpful tools, like smoke detectors, carbon monoxide detectors and fire blankets are put in homes and other buildings where they are needed most. They may share information, with consent, about people at greater risk in a fire for example because they are very elderly, disabled or have dementia; and work together to help these people live more safely."

Source: Website on Scotland community planning https://beta.gov.scot/publications/community-empowerment-scotland-act-2015-part-2-community-planning-plain/

Generally, public councils gather different sectors of civil society, such as academia, civil or community-based organisations and the private sector and local political authorities into a single body. They contribute to the development and implementation of public policies or programmes, including at the local level (Box 2.3).

The main feature that distinguishes councils from other, ad hoc and informal formats of stakeholder participation is their permanent character and clear functions.

If the councils are formed with an objective to act as equal partners to the authority in actual decision-making, they can be considered as a format for engagement, that is, the most intense and collaborative level of stakeholder participation.

Box 2.3. Public councils in Latin American countries

Several countries in Latin America have created local citizen participation bodies – local councils – as a mechanism for citizen participation in development programmes and policies at the municipal level.

Although local councils take on different names and forms across the region, they share common features. The first common feature is composition, meaning that their members represent different sectors of civil society, such as academics, civil society community-based organisations and the private sector. Secondly, they have been formed with a clear link to local political authorities where they have been mandated to collaborative work, such as advising and co-creating public policies or advising and monitoring the design and delivery of public services. Thirdly, public councils typically state their goal as strengthening democracy and improving the quality and responsiveness of public policies, including at the local level.

However, the institutional design of local councils differs across the countries in Latin America. Below are some of the key design features of local councils in the region, focusing on their legal framework, composition, function, and thematic focus.

1. Legal Frameworks

In some cases, the creation of local councils is mandated by the constitution or a national law, while in others, they have emerged at the initiative of local governments and citizens.

The region's laws regulate the different features of the local councils, such as their administration, responsibilities and decision making power, though to varying degrees.

Mexico is an example of a regulatory obligation, as local governments must promote citizen participation and create enabling contexts for the creation of local councils; for example, its National Water Law mandates the creation of Basin Councils.

2. Composition and Function

Evidence from Latin America illustrates the importance of the capacity and will of the actors involved in the councils, especially the local governments' open attitude towards citizen participation. A study demonstrates a link between the

---

capacity of local governments in elaborating plans and policies, and the involvement of citizens in the decision making process. The study found that when local governments had less capacity, they had more confrontational relationships with their citizens.

3. Thematic or general development?

In Latin American countries, there are two different models used: councils are either formed around a thematic focus, such as social policy or environmental preservation, or, alternatively, they guide local development more generally. In the latter case, local councils mainly discuss development plans that cut across many sectors of urban and territorial development.

Source: Perron, M. (2012) ELLA Policy Brief: Increasing Citizen Participation in Local Governance: Latin Americas Local Citizen Councils. ELLA, Practical Action Consulting, Lima, Peru

In short, advisory public councils generally have several advantages as a participation format:

- the Council is established on the basis of a legislative act, which provides a good point of reference for both officials and stakeholders;
- The Council improves transparency of decisions and their dissemination to diverse audiences. If all relevant stakeholders are invited as members to the council, it will have value for the target and interest groups as the creator and provider of transparency in the policy design process;
- The Council is permanent and long-term. The value of the council lies in "shared memory", especially in areas where it is difficult to find active CSOs or individual experts. Gradually, council members come to share common knowledge and information. Shared memory is essential for analysing policies and making justified choices.
- The Council allows for reaching the highest form of participation in which stakeholders can influence decisions. However, the right to decide on policies does not really fall within their mandate, as this responsibility lies with the elected bodies (Noor, K., Uus, M, 2011).

Public Councils in Kazakhstan

In Kazakhstan, according to the law, public councils are "advisory and supervisory entities established by ministries, central executive bodies not part of the Government of the Republic of Kazakhstan, bodies immediately subordinate and accountable to the President of the Republic, as well as bodies attached to local governments." (Law on Public Councils).

Each public institution has to establish a public council. At present, 229 public councils have been established in the Republic of Kazakhstan, including 16 councils at the national level (ministries and the Agency for Civil Service Affairs and Anti-Corruption), 17 at the regional level *(oblast)* and in Astana and Almaty cities, and 196 councils in towns and local districts (Ministry for Social Development).[1]

More than 4,000 people are members of public councils. According to regulation, two thirds of members must represent civil society.[2]

The category of civil society representatives on the public councils is broadly defined, and could include business associations as well as political parties. The remaining 1/3 of the representatives on the public councils are government officials.

The aim of all public councils is to provide a voice to civil society to express the opinion on important social issues. In general, the activity of the Public Council implies monitoring of the activities of state bodies. Decisions and proposals by the Public Councils are advisory in nature, but they are obligatory for consideration by state bodies and require a reasoned response from the state body (Box 2.4).

Box 2.4. Public Council activities

In practical terms, the law lists duties that public councils are expected to fulfil as follows:

- discuss draft budget programs, draft strategic plans or regional development programs, draft state and governmental programs;
- discuss budget program performance, implementation and results of strategic plans or regional development programs, state and governmental programs;
- discuss executive bodies' reports on progress against target indicators;
- discuss reports of the budget program administrator in regard to the implementation of budget programs, implementation of revenue and expenditure plans in connection with the selling of goods (works, services), on the revenue and expenditure in connection with charity;
- participate in the development and discussion of draft legal acts regarding the rights, liberties and duties of citizens;
- consider appeals lodged by natural and legal persons regarding the improvement of public administration and ensuring transparency of the state operations, including the observance of the regulations of service ethics;
- develop and discuss with authorities proposals on the improvement of the legislation of the Republic of Kazakhstan;
- carry out public control in other forms as prescribed by this Law.

Source: Law on Public Councils, as amended on July 11, 2017 (in Russian) http://kazkenes.kz/laws

---

The Public Council makes recommendations to the relevant state body, which considers the recommendations and provides an official answer according to a set deadline (responding in 30 days).

Public councils also have the right to access public information and present requests concerning operations of public institutions at the central or local government level, according to the Law on Access to Information.

An analysis conducted by the Ministry of Religious Affairs and Civil Society in 2017 showed that public councils are becoming involved in reviewing and commenting on a wide range of issues regarding the quality of public services, housing, public transportation, roads improvement, the formation and execution of budgets of different levels, the implementation of development programs of territories, and other topics (Box 2.5).[3]

Box 2.5. Examples of the activities of public councils in Kazakhstan

In Zhambyl Oblast, as a result of direct intervention by the public council for the farmers of the villages "Кеңес" and "Shahan", the issue of running water was solved, the necessary amount was allocated from the regional budget, and more than 3 thousand hectares of irrigated lands were transferred to the population for use.

In Almaty, as a result of monitoring by the public council, gaps in the schedules of public transport have been identified. As a result, a new timetable for public transport was developed and implemented.

In Kostanai Oblast, based on the results of monitoring conducted by the public councils, additional funds were allocated to repair roads in the city of Kostanay, to repair the heating mains of the Fedorovsky District, and to cross the Toguzak River in the Karabalyksky District.

According to the recommendation of the Public Council, Karaganda region established and operates an office to monitor the progress of construction of residential buildings.

In the Syrdarya and Shielinsky districts of Kyzylorda Oblast, members of public councils carried out monitoring of issues of sanitary cleaning, construction, and repair of roads.

Source: Methodological guide for implementing public monitoring, Ministry for Social Development, website consulted in May 2018 https://akk.diakom.gov.kz/ru/content/obshchestven

---

Procedural arrangements for Public Councils' work

As stated in Article 13 of the law on public councils, it is up to the respective council within each public institution to determine the terms and procedures for the arrangement of council meetings and the decision-making process, the selection of the civil society members to the council and the timeframe for their selection, and the list of documents, powers and other issues related to the activities of the working group. The Law does not specify how to finance council activities. The practical arrangements for meetings, office and equipment are compensated by the budget of the public institution with which the council is affiliated. Council members and any expert groups formed on an ad-hoc basis on a specific task work on a volunteer basis.

As the law does not standardise the way that public councils are formed, or the procedures for carrying out their tasks, each council has adopted its own internal working order, specifying the arrangement of meetings and the decision-making process. However, the Ministry of Social Development has produced a draft methodological guide with a recommended template for the internal working order of Public Councils.[4] This is not obligatory, rather a set of recommendations for the selection procedures of members, carrying out council meetings, decision-making procedures and communication with public authorities.

The Ministry of Social Development has analysed the current practice in the councils. In collaboration with representatives of public councils, a set of amendments has been prepared to propose more detailed norms in the regulation to enhance the effectiveness of public councils.[5]

The Ministry has also elaborated a methodological guide[6] to give specific guidance on implementing the function of public monitoring.

In complement to these recommendations in the methodological guide, the OECD suggests the following proposals for consideration with a view to raising the legitimacy of Councils' constitution and improving their operations.

1. **Ensure the representativeness of citizens in local bodies for achieving a balanced composition in council membership.**

The current regulations do not provide specifications about the composition and selection criteria for council members. The current law requires that at least 2/3 of the members of the public council come from civil society. However, the concept of civil society is broad in its nature and does not set clear limits for defining the groups that can act as representatives of civil society.

In discussions, criticism was voiced about persons who have previously been politicians or held high-level positions in public service, and doubts were expressed about their ability to represent the voice of citizens and civil society.

While there should not be any formal barriers to such persons joining the councils, it is advisable to strive for diversity in the council composition. This can be addressed in the selection process. The selection procedure should be formalised by setting up explicit criteria that will be used to consider candidates. Such criteria may include candidate's experience in a relevant field, and a clear connection to constituents in the community whose interests the candidate is representing. Inclusiveness should be ensured further by inviting candidates and selecting public opinion leaders from organisations protecting rights of gender groups, rural residents, ethnic, religions, and other minorities, people with disabilities, and youth.

To ensure accountability, observers can be invited during selection of public council members.

2. **Include criteria and the grounds for terminating the membership status. These criteria could be foreseen in the law.**

Another challenge concerns the need to balance individual members' contribution to the operational work of the council.

Feedback from interviews with councils shows that council members cannot always prioritise the need to attend meetings and participate in discussions in the local council. That means an unequal workload in the council, with some members carrying a bigger burden, which creates tensions.

The proposed amendment to the Law on Public Councils allows any council to decide on the termination of a membership term in case of negligence or at a member's own request to leave the council.[7]

3. **Establish procedures on how to reach a common decision.**

While it is preferable to reach consensus through discussions, there may be cases where voting is advised. In order to carry out open and reliable decision making, it is essential to describe the standard procedure for taking collective decisions, and if needed in specific cases, criteria for making exceptions. These procedures can be described in the internal statute of every council. The ministry has made recommendations on establishing decision-making procedures in its methodological guide, but it is unclear if councils have adopted the recommended approach.

4. Improve the financial autonomy of councils

Consider financial support to compensate the costs of public councils in procuring external expertise, getting legal advice, carrying out site visits or employing other methods to ensure quality input in reviewing normative acts and assessing the impact on the local communities.[8]

5. Strengthen the transparency of the public councils.

The transparency of council's proceedings and work results can be enhanced with the proactive publication of information.

According to a survey carried out by Kazakhstan Citizens Alliance (accessed via the Ministry for Social Development website), the general public puts a premium on receiving information about the work results of the public councils and consequently, how they have affected decision-making by authorities.

The same study showed that the most effective source of information for the public is social networks.

In general, councils are not autonomous in their communication channels. They customarily use websites and social media channels provided by the public authority. While the legal requirement by law has thus been complied with by making general information available, the recommendation is to enhance usability and create trust by maintaining autonomous channels for the council to inform and interact with its constituents, the citizens (Box 2.6).

Box 2.6. Sharing information with the public

The city administration of Almaty is giving advice to citizens how to present requests for information to the city or any public authorities.

Similar simple and visual guide gives a step-by-step guidance for citizens how to interact with authorities to obtain answers to their questions, proposals and initiatives.

In a year, over 120,000 applications were sent by citizens through social networks, thematic sites, by reception hours, helplines and letters.

As public councils have a role in facilitating citizen-to-government interaction, the councils could establish a similar guide on their site or social media channel to instruct and assist citizens to formulate their request and send it to the department that is responsible for managing this request.

Source: Website of the Public Council of Almaty city, https://open-almaty.kz/ru/kak-napravit-obrashcheniezhalobu-v-akimat

---

The role of stakeholder participation in ensuring transparent and inclusive regulation

Transparency is one of the central pillars of good regulative framework supporting accountability of government, sustaining confidence in the legal environment, making regulations more accessible, less influenced by special interests, and therefore more conducive to competition, trade and investment. To ensure transparency, public institutions need to take several actions, including standardised procedures for making and changing regulations, consultation with stakeholders, effective communication and publication of regulations and plain language drafting, codification, controls on administrative discretion, and effective appeals mechanisms. This may involve a mix of formal and informal processes.

The OECD's approach to transparency in regulatory process is framed in the OECD Council Recommendation on Regulation Policy and Governance (OECD 2012), which states, inter alia, the following principles:

Governments should establish a clear policy identifying how open and balanced public consultation in the process of rule-making will take place.

Governments should cooperate with stakeholders on reviewing existing and developing new regulations by:

- Actively engaging all relevant stakeholders during the regulation-making process and designing consultation processes to maximise the quality of the information received and its effectiveness.
- Consulting on all aspects of impact assessment analysis and using, for example, impact assessments as part of the consultation process;
- Making available to the public, as far as possible, all relevant material from regulatory dossiers including the supporting analyses, and the reasons for regulatory decisions as well as all relevant data.
- All regulations should be easily accessible by the public. A complete and up-to-date legislative and regulatory database should be freely available to the public in a searchable format through a user-friendly interface over the Internet.
- Governments should have a policy that requires regulatory texts to be drafted using plain language. They should also provide clear guidance on compliance with regulations, making sure that affected parties understand their rights and obligations" (OECD, 2012).

Analysis of the public control functions

In the Kazakhstan law of public councils, Articles 16-19 lay out the procedures for public councils in the form of **public control.** The forms of public control are defined as follows:

1. Public expertise: the procedure for reviewing draft normative acts for compliance with public interests.
2. Public monitoring: the procedure for monitoring the activities of state bodies by public councils, as well as non-profit organisations, citizens on behalf of public councils.
3. Public hearings: public discussion of issues, socially significant decisions of state bodies on the issue of their conformity to public interests.
4. Discussion of the report on the results of work of state bodies: public discussion at the meeting of the Public Council of the results of the activities of state bodies and local, self-government bodies.

Public expertise function

The OECD Guiding Principles for Open and Inclusive Policy Making emphasise that participation means that all stakeholders should have equal opportunities and multiple channels to access information, and also, that they should be consulted.

OECD experience shows that consultation on laws and regulations improves the quality of rules and programmes, increases compliance, and reduces the enforcement costs for both governments and citizens subject to the rules. If carried out successfully, the process of making citizens' opinions heard can empower the population (OECD, 2003).

One of the major tasks entrusted by the law to public councils is to review draft legal acts with a view to considering the rights, freedoms and duties of citizens. This function corresponds to the concept of **public consultation**, which is a commonly used method for authorities to receive feedback on proposed legislation or policy measures.

In order to illustrate the scale of carrying out this function by public councils in Kazakhstan, statistics show that in 2017, more than nine thousand draft normative acts were published in the central portal Open Legislation https://legalacts.egov.kz/. Approximately one tenth of them included comments provided by public councils (source: Ministry for Social Development).

How public consultation works in Kazakhstan

The wider public has the possibility to comment on draft regulations once they are uploaded on the website of the ministry in charge or at the central portal Open Legislation. Anyone, including the members of the council, has ten working days to comment on the draft proposal. This period is relatively short and, in the case of complex or extensive legislation, it might not allow for a thorough analysis of the potential impact or the formulation of an informed opinion by council members. In comparison, in OECD countries with mandatory consultation periods, stakeholders have on average of four to six weeks to provide their comments.

Comments made by the council require a written reply by the concerned institution. Councils follow the same procedure as the general public for commenting on draft regulations once they are uploaded onto the central Open Legislation portal. The draft regulation is generally available in both Kazakh and Russian. Comments can be made in either language. There is neither a specific consultation period nor a concrete call for comments; only contact details are provided. Throughout the development of the draft regulation, citizens have the opportunity to provide comments while the online version is updated as the draft changes. For the moment, only the draft itself and not its accompanying documents, such as the regulatory impact assessment, is posted online.

According to regulation adopted by the order of the Minister of Information and Communications in 2016, the authority must consider the comments within three working days after the completion of the public discussion on the central Open Legislation portal and take decisions on their acceptance or rejection, specifying the reasons. Whereas the government is thus reportedly responsive to comments, the practices, e.g. the format of giving feedback, have not yet been established. This feedback needs to be monitored by public councils to verify whether or not the proposed changes have been adopted.

If the draft regulation were to impact businesses, Atameken, the National Business Association, must also be consulted, as it plays a special partnership role to the government in the process of preparing draft normative acts. Membership in the Chamber is obligatory for subjects registered for business in Kazakhstan, excluding those that are subject to mandatory membership in the other non-commercial organisations and state bodies.

The law describes activities of the Atameken for the collection, systematisation, analysis and compilation of information, including the assessment of the extent to which tasks have been performed and problems solved, an evaluation of the intended solution of the normative legal act, as well as its influence on entrepreneurship in the Republic of Kazakhstan.

Atameken has an obligation to actively participate in public consultations on new draft laws regarding the business environment. This includes regulations at either the central government or subnational level. It also has a right to initiate reviews of existing regulations. Public council can also initiate monitoring of current legislation, with an aim to provide feedback on its effects on citizens' wellbeing. In that case, the findings and proposals to amend the law have advisory nature.

As the law gives Atameken a mandate to review and assess the potential impact of draft legislation, this organisation has a remarkable influence on legislation.

A special procedure is in place for draft laws that have an effect on private businesses. In this case the explanatory note must include an estimate of the costs for businesses, and the draft and explanatory note must be sent to representative organisations for comment.

The business associations also have direct access to the working process, obtain information, and are present in committees who work on sector policies and legislation.

As an example, in Western Kazakhstan, members of Atameken are part of more than 50% of thematic committees formed by the regional administration. This means that they are involved in the drafting process from the early stages of developing normative acts or any other types of regulation.

Thus, the role of Atameken differs from the role of other public councils, which obtain access to the content of acts only when the draft is disclosed to the general public, shortly before the final decision is adopted.

Atameken plays an important role in ensuring the transparency of the legislation-making process. By publishing their comments on the central website Open Legislation (as part of the egov.kz portal), the information on their position and proposals becomes available to all other stakeholders, including members of the public council. Atameken's analysis and proposal work is performed by professional legal advisers and experts on business sectors. This makes their contribution an additional and valuable source of information for the members of public councils or any individual who preparing his/her own comments on legislative drafts.

Viewing consultation as an integral part of the regulatory process is a good way to organise internal processes in the public institution and coordinate the tasks of civil servants with various responsibilities within these processes. Secondly, it enhances the motivation of public councils and other civil society stakeholders who need to clearly understand their role and working process in making their contribution. However, it should be recalled that public consultation cannot substitute a fully-fledged regulatory impact assessment carried out by public officials or commissioned from external experts such as researchers or private sector professionals.

Box 2.7. Better Regulation practice by the European Commission

In May 2015, the European Commission adopted its "Better Regulation Package", outlining measures to deliver better rules for better results. The measures aim to prepare policies inclusively, based on full transparency and engagement, including by consulting more and listening more carefully to the views of those affected by legislation.

As a key part of the package of reforms, citizens and stakeholders will have an increased opportunity to provide their views over the entire lifecycle of a policy. They can provide feedback on "roadmaps" and "inception impact assessments", which integrates citizen and stakeholder feedback at the beginning of the policy cycle. Furthermore, twelve weeks of open public consultations take place when preparing new proposals or evaluating existing policies. Consultations are mandatory for new proposals with significant impacts and optional for proposals without significant impacts.

The Commission systematically conducts impact assessments of major initiatives. The purpose of impact assessments is to search for the best mix of instruments based on the available evidence. A range of policy options are compared to the problem at hand and the objectives to be achieved on the basis of the best evidence available, including stakeholder consultation.

After the Commission has adopted a proposal, citizens and stakeholders are invited to provide feedback, which will be presented to the European Parliament and Council to feed into the further legislative debate.

For each initiative, a consultation strategy must be established, identifying relevant stakeholders and the most appropriate consultation activities and methods to target stakeholders in the most effective way. The strategy must include an open public consultation when required (see above) and may include, among other activities, targeted consultations, surveys, focus groups, workshops or conferences. The web portal "Your Voice in Europe" provides a single access point for all open public consultations and feedback opportunities.

In addition, a new "Lighten the Load – Have Your Say" feature on the Commission's better regulation website gives everyone a chance to air their views and make comments on existing EU laws and initiatives in addition to the formal consultations the Commission undertakes.

Source: The Governance of Inclusive Growth. An overview of country initiatives. OECD (2016). More information on EC Better Regulation Toolbox and an overview of consultation tools http://ec.europa.eu/smart-regulation/guidelines/toc_tool_en.htm.

In its 2014 Review on Regulatory Policy in Kazakhstan, the OECD made a recommendation to "Improve the consultation process via the ministries' advisory councils in order to increase stakeholder participation, and adopt a more pro-active approach to public consultation" (OECD, 2014).

The recommendation addressed the finding that "the benefit of public consultation is hindered by very short deadlines with respect to councils and the procedure for more general public consultation lacks explicit calls for comments, clear timelines and guidance." (OECD, 2014). The process of public consultation has not been substantially improved since then.

Revising the procedural arrangements for the step-by-step flow of the regulatory process is a good way to set commonly agreed-upon standards for consultation that set forth the concrete stages and procedures for including the input of external stakeholders, such as public councils and business associations, into the drafting of normative acts.

For example, in Estonia, as in several other EU countries, the procedures for carrying out impact assessments and including stakeholder participation in the regulatory process (public consultation) have been streamlined as procedural steps in the policy-making process (Box 2.8). It would be advisable to illustrate the process description visually to communicate the participation options for stakeholders.

Box 2.8. Participation in the regulatory process in Estonia

It is a common understanding that in good policy making and legislation, anyone affected by the legislation has an opportunity to express their opinion, whether as a citizen, a non-governmental partner or an expert. In addition, policy-making requires the collaboration of several government actors. Stakeholder participation is guided by the Good Practices of Participation.

Good Practices is not a normative act, but a set of obligatory recommendations from Centre of Government to all public authorities, and especially for those who are preparing regulation or policy documents that require government decisions.

Process description

Initiating legislation

At a political level, or in the ministry, for example, there may be a perceived social problem that needs to be addressed, or an opportunity that needs to be explored.

Identification of a problem or opportunity may start from, for example, policy analysis, a pre-election promise, monitoring and analysing applied practices, media articles or some other way, for example, if stakeholders signal that there is a bottleneck in implementing the law in practice. The initiative can also be submitted on the basis of a collective appeal, or petition (Note that collective petitioning is regulated by law in Estonia).

As the first step, it is necessary to understand the extent of the problem or possibility (including who is affected by the situation and in what way) and its nature (whether the problem permanent or temporary, whether it has existed for a long time or is a new phenomenon, and whether it concerns interaction between levels of government or between government and citizens). Often, problems can have several parallel aspects; therefore, all relationships with affected stakeholders need to be well mapped out. Note that the "problem" may actually be an opportunity, e.g. to improve the business environment, which the government intervention can facilitate, and, therefore, the problem deserves consideration.

In the broadest sense, the government's activities are governed by the Government's programme and strategies, while the need for change may also arise from another source,

---

for example, the adoption or implementation of EU law, or problems that have been brought to the attention of the Parliament by interest groups.

Concept paper

Depending on the need to explore proposed changes before making an actual regulation, the policy maker can use the Green Paper, which is an initial proposal for a strategic plan or a new piece of legislation and presents an analysis of the problem.

At this stage, it is very important that experts, non-governmental partners and citizens become involved in the debate.

To make the most of this opportunity to participate, stakeholders need to know what decisions are being prepared. This information is available from the government's program, the overview of ministries' legislative initiatives, as well as each ministry's work plans.

Good practice of participation foresees that a government institution submits a draft law, a draft development plan, or any other initiative with a significant effect for public consultation in the central government information system (EIS). If necessary, the material should be sent directly to interested stakeholders, asking for their proposals and the publishing of opinions, explaining why their comments are needed, what they can expect regarding the feedback by government, and the further process for this legislation until its adoption.

Any additional information should be sought from the official in charge of preparing a specific decision. In addition, all ministries have appointed a coordinator, a specialist who can be contacted if there are more questions about organising stakeholder participation by government institutions.

Note: Translated from original (Estonian). Website accessed in May 2018, https://riigikantselei.ee/et/poliitikakujundamise-ja-oigusloome-protsess

Source: Opportunities for stakeholder participation in the regulatory process. The material has been created by the Strategy Unit in the Government Office to provide an overview of how policies are being prepared and laws are being drafted, and how non-governmental stakeholders can participate in these processes.

Recommendations on improving the public expertise (consultation) function

- Integrate the collection of stakeholders' input in the formal process flow of designing and adopting normative acts. The guidance to conduct consultation during legislative process can be adopted without changing the relevant laws on Public Councils and on Business Associations. Formulate detailed guidelines to carry out public consultation as a common format for collecting stakeholders' input in legislation and regularly offer training to civil servants and public councils to ensure their implementation.
- Proactively advertise online consultation for the wider public. An open call for contributions includes setting clear timelines for giving input, specifying what questions are open for discussion, and describing the decision-making process following the consultation.
- Consider creating a concise feedback report on every completed consultation. Encourage a good practice to report on how external stakeholders have influenced

the regulation by highlighting amendments in the final draft of the legal act that were based on stakeholder input.

Public monitoring function

Public monitoring as stated by the Law on Public Councils involves monitoring and analysing the activities of state bodies by the Councils by taking into account the opinion of citizens, citizens' appeals, proposals of chairmen and secretaries of Public Councils, representatives of non-profit organisations and participants in training seminars held in the regions.

Public monitoring procedures are conducted with the aim of determining the quality of public services, the implementation of government programs, budget programs and other development programs that determine the norms of legislation by state bodies or their representatives. Public monitoring can be initiated upon a request placed to the Council by an individual citizen or by the decision of the Council itself.

To perform this procedure, the Public Councils are authorised to request the necessary information from state bodies, within the scope of the monitoring subject and the procedure established in Kazakhstan's law on access to information.

To receive all relevant information, the Public Council may set up meetings with public officials. It can also contract an external expert or set up an ad-hoc task group to gather evidence and analyse the challenges of the current situation. The task group then draws up conclusions based on the results of the monitoring. The public council conducts a meeting to discuss the findings and make its recommendations and proposals to the public authority.

The format of the public monitoring is similar to that of an audit, as the objective is to identify gaps and problems in the current implementation of policies, or deficiencies in the delivery and quality of public services.

It remains outside the scope of the Councils' mandate and voluntary contribution to follow the same process as that of an official internal or external performance audit.

It may be useful to learn from the concept of citizen audits, which usually focus on certain aspects of a public service, without aiming to provide a comprehensive assessment or full-fledged performance audit (Box 2.9).

Box 2.9. Citizen audits in the Philippines

In participatory, or citizen auditing processes, citizens (civil society, academic groups, community members, private sector) and the government work together to audit the delivery public services and government programs.

Citizen audit utilises various data-gathering and performance assessment methods like surveys, interviews, quality tests, collation of statistics, review of records, case studies, and participant observation. A key concern in social audits is how resources were used to attain social objectives.

In the Philippines, the supreme audit institution was the agency that adopted citizen audit approaches to complement its existing public auditing procedures. They have carried out participatory audit processes on topics like flood control, solid waste management, health programs and hygiene in schools.

The components of the program are described as follows:

- Partnership Building - Terms of engagement among stakeholders are established through a consultative and collaborative approach.
- Capacity Development - This activity builds the capacity of primary stakeholders, mainly civil society actors, auditors, and other government officials to undertake participatory audits. For greater effectiveness, capacity building is carried out in actual work situations to focus on improving practice.
- Public Communication - An integrated communication plan is designed to create awareness of the program, and generate support from internal and external stakeholders.
- Knowledge and Tools Generation -To facilitate knowledge sharing and ensure that best practices are replicated, the experiences of civil society organisations and government agencies are documented into case studies

Analysing the experiences of citizen audit processes that have been implemented so far, the audit institution highlights directions for improvement in the follow-up of auditing processes, ensuring that interested citizen groups can work together to monitor actions taken on public audit reports and recommendations. They also find challenges in sustaining public focus on the audit process, and keeping the stakeholders updated on the audited programs.

Source: website of Affiliated Network for Social Accountability in East Asia and the Pacific, http://www.ansa-eap.net/projects/citizen-participatory-audit/

Recommendations for improving the public monitoring function

To create a more streamlined procedure for conducting public monitoring, the adoption of good practices to facilitate an uptake of monitoring results should be considered:

- make concrete proposals that are in accordance with the goals and objectives as described in official documents about the social issue in question;
- present recommendations in writing, in a brief and to-the-point manner, that highlight the proposed measures to address the problems identified in the course of monitoring;

- assess the economic feasibility of proposed changes by evaluating the workload and cost associated with implementing the proposed solution;
- point to best practices in solving similar problems in other regions or towns;
- collect evidence from on-site visits and consult the local community to define the situation;
- request comments from community stakeholders on the preliminary recommendations.

Public hearing function

Public hearings are held at the initiative of the Public Council. The public hearings take the form of a meeting at which various questions are raised for public discussion regarding the budget, draft strategic plans or development programs for territories, planned state and government programs regarding compliance with the norms of service ethics and other publicly significant issues related to the work of government agencies. Also, public hearings can be organised by the public council with the presence of senior public officials in preparation of comments on draft normative legal acts regarding the rights, freedoms and duties of citizens, and to consider appeals of citizens and legal entities on improving the public administration work.

Public hearings are recorded and an official memo is drafted. The decision of the meeting is considered valid for consideration if at least half of the present members of the Public Council have voted in favour of the decision. The protocol containing all comments, suggestions and recommendations is then sent to the relevant state bodies, and published in the media and on the relevant Internet sites.

Box 2.10. The implementation of the public hearing function by the public council at the Ministry of Interior

The council initiated three public hearings in 2016 and another three in 2017, inviting a diverse range of participants such as representatives of international organisations and diplomatic missions, in addition to civil society and government agencies. The topics under discussion ranged from preventing drug abuse in the penitentiaries to improving relationships between citizens and the police.

The briefing memos were drawn up, including council's recommendation for further steps by authorities.

Source: Report on Public Council activities prepared by the Chairman of the Council (in hard copy)

Recommendations on improving the public hearing function

To create a more standardised procedure for conducting public hearings similar to the public monitoring function, it may be worthwhile to consider:

- Based on discussions and recommendations emerging from hearings, to make concrete proposals for further action, in order to ensure implementation by relevant authorities.
- Follow up implementation of proposals from public hearings by regularly asking the authorities about the progress made in improving the situation. Failing to follow

up and track progress means that the public hearings do not perform a public control function and instead become thematic seminars with a low accountability effect.

Innovative forms of stakeholder participation

Previously, a ladder of participation was used as a way to describe the intensity and depth of interaction of citizens and civil society groups with government. The highest level is engagement, when citizens are actively involved with authorities in defining the process and content of policy. In these cases, citizens co-create the final decision, which is why the approach is also known as co-creation.

Co-creation requires that government be open about the results and not have a pre-defined agenda or political agreement that frames the question to be solved. In such a case, citizens' proposals provide an important contribution to formulating policy options, and potentially deciding on the final policy solution, the final distribution of public funds, or the final design of the public service to be launched.

Across the world, different methods of crowdsourcing citizens' proposals are used to collect feedback for amending legislation, plan local development, or debate a controversial social issue to define potential policy interventions. In many cases, digital channels are used in the process of gathering proposals and collectively deliberating on their merits (Box 2.11).

An indicator of real citizen engagement is the willingness of authorities to give participants the power to influence the final decision. This mandate also becomes a responsibility for those persons who take part in formulating the outcomes.

The method of participatory budgeting is widely used in different parts of the world to make decisions on a communal, municipal or institutional budget.

Box 2.11. Citizens engage directly with Parliament

In France, a non-Government initiative makes it possible for citizens to go online to engage with parliamentarians as they develop legislation. The Parliament and Citizens platform, operated by the non-partisan association "Démocratie Ouverte", enables parliamentarians to publish a short video and text outlining a problem they would like to address and the solutions they propose. This includes resources for the citizens to access and learn more about the issue in question. Citizens then have an opportunity to vote for or against the proposal, present their arguments, make counter-proposals and identify their favourite comments. After 30 days, the consultation closes and the site displays cards showing different comments – comments "for" are showing in green, comments "against" are shown in red. Démocratie Ouverte synthesises the results and hosts a public debate on Google Hangouts between the MP and active participants randomly selected or chosen by vote. Then, the parliamentarian posts a new video in which they propose a bill in parliament, accompanied by an explanation of what choices they made as a result of the consultation process.

Finland has developed a pilot project for an online "opinions service" of experts and citizens (lausuntopalvelu.fi) to comment, discuss, consult, and browse to assess and improve regulations.

The Latvian government founded "manabalss.lv" as an open government initiative that allows citizens to propose a petition online, which then is refined with experts for further consultation.

Source: The Governance of Inclusive Growth. An overview of country initiatives. OECD (2016). More information and guidelines which promote participatory mechanisms: www.cnle.gouv.fr/Guides-et-supports-methodologiques.html

---

Participatory budgeting can be defined as a decision-making process through which citizens deliberate and negotiate the distribution of public resources. It is envisioned as a grassroots endeavour, including community self-organisation and decision-making. By participating, local residents discuss their collective needs and decide which projects to fund. The method focuses on identifying demands in a community and setting their own priorities for funding (Box 2.12).

Co-creation denotes a collaborative process in which diverse stakeholders take part and become responsible for the end result.

Just as involvement in any participatory process is voluntary, so too is partaking in a co-creation effort. The aim of co-creation is to produce "actionable knowledge" – decisions about what needs to be done about the problem and how to do it. These results can include a joint action plan or an agreement to redistribute funds, for example. Neither co-creation nor participation are ends in themselves; both processes aim for an outcome that is the product of the collaborative effort of those involved (Prager K. 2016).

2. ANALYSIS AND RECOMMENDATIONS | **43**

Box 2.12. Citizens distribute funds by participatory budgeting

Iceland, the City of Reykjavík

Iceland has, since 2012, actively offered various options to enhance public participation in deliberative democracy and decision making via two initiatives:

Better Reykjavik is an online consultation forum where citizens are given the chance to present their ideas on issues regarding services and operations of the City of Reykjavík.

Better Districts is a collaborative project between citizens and administrative authorities for prioritising and distributing funds for new projects on a smaller scale and projects of maintenance in the districts of Reykjavík. This project is intended to enhance public participation in deliberative democracy and democratic decision making, by giving citizens the role to propose and select public objects to be developed with the public resources.

Paris, France

Since 2014 the municipality of Paris gives its citizens the opportunity to decide on the use of 5% of its investment budget, which amounts to EUR 0.5 billion in 2014-20. The aim is to involve citizens in municipal politics to promote social cohesion and to learn their preferences. It builds on the principles of open government and promotes a stronger relation between citizens, their representatives and the public institutions. The project tries to harness creative ideas of Parisians, and the process is as follows:

1. Parisians propose their ideas for investment projects on a website;

2. The municipality evaluates the feasibility of the proposals; and

3. Project proposals are submitted to vote by Parisians.

Source: The Governance of Inclusive Growth. An overview of country initiatives, OECD (2016) and Towards an Open Government in Kazakhstan OECD (2017)

Co-creation is more likely to be successful if there is genuine interest in a community, not just the initiative of government to find actionable proposals (Box 2.13).

Box 2.13. Co-creating accessibility legislation in Canada

In 2016 to 2017, the newly appointed Minister responsible for persons with disabilities in Canada set up a large-scale and truly inclusive consultation on disability issues. The results were used to create new federal accessibility legislation.

Canadians were encouraged to share their ideas and were offered many different opportunities to do so. In-person public meetings were held across the country that was supported by local leaders from the disability community. Participants were also invited to share their ideas by email, phone or by sending audio or video recordings.

- Over 4,300 people answered questions online and over 200 people shared their ideas via letters, emails, videos or phone.

- Over 90 reports were provided by disability organizations, unions, businesses and other levels of government.

- Over 1,400 people participated in 18 in-person meetings held across Canada.

- One hundred and fifteen youth from across the country attended a one-day Youth Forum hosted by the Minister. These young leaders with disabilities worked together to share their ideas.

- Over 110 experts attended thematic roundtables hosted by the Minister on disability issues. At these meetings, specific accessibility topics were discussed such as how to make public spaces, transport and customer service more accessible.

To start the co-creation, the Government prepared a number of open-ended questions, including:

- What should be the goal of the new legislation?

- What accessibility barriers should be included?

- How do we make sure the new legislation is being followed?

- In addition to the new legislation, how should we better promote accessibility?

- How do we ensure that all Canadians are informed on a regular basis if the new legislation is working, or if it needs to be improved?

Throughout the process, people shared their stories, describing the barriers that were currently leaving them out of full inclusion in society. One of the most significant areas of exclusion has been around personal decision-making. This includes being given the opportunity to have a choice regarding personal matters such as where to live, what medical procedures to have, how to save and spend money, whom to marry and whether or not to have children. Canadians with disabilities have also been excluded from government programs, policies and laws that impact their lives. While there was agreement on many overarching ideas, there were also different opinions about how the new legislation could work. Participants also discussed areas where the federal, provincial and territorial governments share some responsibilities. For example, participants discussed how accessibility interacts with issues of poverty, housing, education and health care. It was committed that what was learned from the consultation would be shared across all levels of government.

Participants were asked about the ways the Government of Canada could monitor organizations to make sure they are following the new legislation. Most thought that a range of tools should be used and that people with disabilities should also be involved in the monitoring process. These tools included:

- Action plans – The legislation could require organizations to make action plans that describe how they will improve their accessibility over time.

- Progress reports – The legislation could require organizations to report on what they are doing to improve accessibility.

- Reviews – The legislation could describe how the Government would check the action plans and reports that organizations provide.

- Complaints – The legislation could describe how Canadians could make complaints if they think that an organization is not following the legislation.

Source: Government of Canada website, Accessible Canada - Creating new federal accessibility legislation: What we learned from Canadians https://www.canada.ca/en/employment-social-development/programs/planned-accessibility-legislation/reports/consultations-what-we-learned.html

Resources and institutional framework to support stakeholder participation

Besides monitoring compliance with the legislation and making amendments to address gaps in implementation, there is a need for a supportive role in motivating, guiding and advising government agencies in how to plan, implement and evaluate stakeholder participation. The supporting role should be mandated to the government institution or institutions in charge of promoting the implementation of open government principles of transparency and citizen participation.

In Kazakhstan, the Ministry of Information and Communications is responsible for overseeing the implementation of the Law on Access to Information and publication of government information, while the Ministry for Social Development is tasked with ensuring stakeholder participation opportunities and supporting the work of Public Councils. There is thus the need for co-ordinating activities between them.

Both ministries play a role in coordinating with other public institutions on the implementation of Public Councils as a mechanism in their policy-making processes.

The best way to achieve a systematic working method is to institutionalise a coordination function, by agreeing on distinct responsibilities and establishing a regular format for information exchange and collective decision-making. Alternatively, a special function or position can be created to act as a central co-ordinator for Open Government activities.

Box 2.14. Coordination of Open Government in Finland

In Finland a specific coordination structure has been created in order to increase co-operation within the government and between different administrative branches in the area of transparency and civic participation. A ministerial democracy network has been established in order to increase co-ordination between the ministries operating in the field. The network consists of civil servants from all ministries. The networks task is to draft and monitor democracy policy within the government. The network monitors the development of legislation in the field of transparency and participation, exchange information and initiate new development project. The network works in close co-operation with the Finnish Open Government Partnership coordination group, in order to co-ordinate actions in the field and to make coherent policies. Both the aforementioned working groups are represented in the local democracy network maintained by the Association for Municipalities and Regions. The progress is followed up by the Advisory Board on Civil Society Affairs, which is a delegation of Associations and NGO´s appointed by the Government.

Source: Government of Finland

To steer the practical implementation of activities that are foreseen by law, it is worth considering combining open government goals and initiatives into one comprehensive document.

As recommended for Kazakhstan in the Open Government Review (OECD, 2017b),

- Consider developing a comprehensive open government strategy (a single document) that includes principles, long-term goals, medium-term objectives, policy instruments, and initiatives to be carried out to achieve the goals. The strategy could also include indicators to assess the progress of open government initiatives, including the effect of public councils as a participation mechanism.
- To elaborate the strategy, create a working group tasked with preparing the draft strategy and planning relevant activities that lead to desired outcomes. It is important that the working group ensures government and CSO stakeholders' participation and that the discussion and decisions are made available to the public.
- Create "institutional infrastructure" by inviting a group of public officials to act as leaders of open government, and in turn as knowledge brokers for their colleagues.
- Foster collaboration on open government initiatives across agencies, between a variety of relevant offices and positions within agencies, as well as interaction with non-governmental organisations, business, media, and the general public.

In order to support the implementation of current open government practices already foreseen in the regulation, there is a range of activities to be considered. The choice of activities and responsibility for their implementation should be agreed upon by the ministries in charge of the open government agenda.

A selection of activities may include the following:

- Consider financial support (targeted funding) for organisations, including local authorities who undertake innovative or large-scale participation processes that extend beyond the minimum requirements set by the law;

- Carry out regular monitoring and evaluation activities to collect data on the effects of results of participation processes. Monitoring also gives evidence of best practices, which should be rewarded. Outstanding cases should be highlighted publicly and their experience shared with other local authorities and government institutions.

Box 2.15. Institutional support to monitor implementation

The Oversight Committee for the Implementation of Stakeholder Participation as a component of the Estonian Civil Society Development Concept.

The Concept is a document regulating dialogue and collaboration between public sector and CSOs. A multi-stakeholder Committee was formed to serve as a permanent mechanism for monitoring adherence to the principles set in the Concept. Stakeholder participation is one of the principles, with a focus on guiding the planning, implementation and evaluation of public consultation processes.

The Committee has a maximum of 24 members, half of whom are senior civil servants from ministries, while the other half are representatives of CSOs who have been selected through an open competition. The committee is headed by the Minister of the Interior. The Ministry of the Interior also serves as the secretariat of the Committee, organising and hosting the meetings, preparing materials and drafting protocols for discussion and decisions. All Committee materials are public. Press releases are published regularly to highlight the main results achieved in the period of implementing action plans and share decisions made at the meetings, which usually take place twice a year.

The Committee's mandate states that its Civil Society members represent their organisations and target groups. To this end, they have the obligation to convey the materials and decisions they make to the committee to the members and employees of their organisations and to involve them in shaping the views expressed by the Committee.

The committee has a role in setting bi-annual objectives in fostering the improvement of the civic space and the involvement of civil society actors in policy-making and service delivery. It oversees the implementation of action plans designed and applied in the relevant ministries.

One of the Committee's functions is mediation in cases of conflict, which is conducted in accordance with the principles of collaboration as described in the Concept.

The Concept provides that representatives of CSOs and public authorities will observe the principles and values of civic engagement, participation, respect, partnership, responsibility and accountability, political independence of the citizens' initiatives, corruption prevention, sustainable and balanced development, and equal treatment.

Monitoring compliance with the principles is the task of a special working group. The group encourages everyone – be they a civil servant or a citizen – to submit a complaint to report acts contrary to the agreed principles and best practice of cooperation. It is a way to hold the government accountable in case any public institution fails to conduct a transparent and inclusive policy process.

The group does not condemn or punish, but it helps to interpret the principles, assess the submitted case or complaint, and give recommendations for better cooperation.

Source: Website of the Ministry of Interior of Estonia, responsible for Civil Society development (in Estonian) https://www.siseministeerium.ee/et/eesmark-tegevused/kodanikuuhiskond/eesti-kodanikuuhiskonna-arengu-kontseptsioon

Capacity for facilitating stakeholder participation

The existence of regulations, obligations and procedural rules is not enough to ensure that participatory policy-making becomes an everyday practice.

Case studies of public participation have concluded that the success of the participation process depends on the readiness of those who organise and facilitate stakeholder participation (usually officials in public authorities) to go beyond what is required by law, or the specifics of their job description. Ensuring awareness and motivation of stakeholders is a task that should go beyond minimum regulatory requirements.

One of the main prerequisites for participation is that the prospective participants must have access to information that is relevant for decision-making. However, simply granting access to information or making it available is not enough to ensure a good level of engagement. Public participation is an active process, where the person responsible for decision-making seeks active contact with people who are affected by the decision, and who might want to join the discussion.

Good collaborative relations entail an open-minded approach and goodwill from both the officials and the participants.

Box 2.16. The public council as a facilitator of diverse interests

Owing to the intervention by the public council in Ust-Kamenogorsk in Kazakhstan, the department of business activities and the local police service were called to address the issue of unauthorised trade in the central square and in areas of significant traffic congestion.

Discussions were held with all concerned actors, including local administration, the police, entrepreneurs and community representatives. As a result of council activities, a compromise solution was identified to regulate temporary trade in sites with the greatest burden on traffic.

In complicated cases, the council consults with professionals to formulate evidence-based proposals and assess the potential impact of a given decision. For example, the Transport Infrastructure Commission is considering to install an on-demand traffic light at a currently unregulated pedestrian crossing. The problem was raised by means of residents' appeals. The council works with an independent expert to evaluate the consequences of this specific method for regulating the pedestrian crossing.

Source: response by Ust-Kamenogorsk Public Council, OECD survey in June 2018

The stakeholders, citizens and CSO representatives who are willing to commit time to serve on the councils and to participate actively in them are crucial in achieving the objectives that the law is assigning to the public councils.

Other stakeholders should also be invited to take part in all participation formats continuously, as the opportunities created by the law are open to everyone.

Recommendations for public institutions and local authorities to enhance capacities for stakeholder participation

Consider supportive activities, including:

- Make regular training sessions available for local level civil servants on how to conduct participation processes; including practical workshops with the participation of civil servants;
- Create and disseminate written guidelines and manuals on how to conduct participation processes, including the explanation of regulations, steps in policy-making and the role of consultation in the policy process.
- Organise regular meetings and peer-to-peer exchanges between public councils to share good practices.
- Ensure the transparency of law-making, by making sure that all legal acts and policy documents subject to public consultations according to law are published on the central portal.
- Ensure continuous help-desk support (including technical support and advice on practical work procedures) to government agencies, which need advice in setting up consultations, giving feedback and publishing the results of consultations.

Public awareness of the Public Councils' work

It is vital to share information on a council's work process, from publishing the annual work plan to giving regular updates of items on the agenda on a weekly or monthly basis.

The public should also know what feedback the authorities give to council proposals and which questions that they raise with the Akimat or any individual public institution.

Finally, to ensure the council's accountability, it should publish reports of its activities and comment on the results, as well as the lessons learned and challenges of its work. This information is used to monitor and evaluate the council's effectiveness in fulfilling its functions as described by the law. It also enables an assessment of how well the council is responding to expectations of the community that they are representing.

Recommendations on raising awareness of public councils

- Publish information about forthcoming consultations on the respective government and local government web pages. Each government agency is responsible for publishing the legal acts for consultation, and hence, it should also be responsible for promoting the opportunity for the general public to take part in consultations. The opportunities for taking part in consultations should be widely disseminated.
- Monitor user take-up and monitor the rate of adoption of the channel by user groups, i.e. civil servants, invited experts and general public.
- Award regular users of the portal, whether they are civil society contributors or from government agencies, who regularly conduct consultations.
- Use a diverse range of channels to inform the public about participatory processes. It is advisable not to rely only on the central portal. Authorities should also include local media, official Facebook and Twitter accounts used by local authorities, and

collaborate with Civil Society organisations to disseminate information on taking part in pubic consultations.

- Ensure that a summary of the consultation process is published that analyses the input from stakeholders and highlights the changes made on the basis of the consultation input. This serves the purpose of encouraging citizens to interact with authorities, to take part in public hearings and meetings, and propose their own initiatives for local development.

Monitoring and evaluation of the public councils' results and effects of stakeholder participation

By evaluating open government initiatives, including participation mechanisms, the government receives feedback to improve the quality of these initiatives. Evaluation also enables the legitimisation of participation initiatives and prompts accountability for the activities undertaken and the public resources used to implement these activities.

Evaluation serves the objective of motivating citizens to take part in participatory processes, as it is a way to demonstrate the achieved impact.

To assess the results achieved, the process must be documented, and its immediate outputs reported, including the number and nature of proposals received from participants, the number of participants and their demographics, especially the extent to which diversity and inclusiveness goals were reached.

Indicators can also be used to evaluate the performance and results of the Public Councils themselves, such as the one used by the Council of Almaty (Box 2.17).

Box 2.17. Criteria for evaluation of council members' work in the city of Almaty

The Public Council of Almaty city introduced an addendum to the Regulations on the Organisation of the Public Council, by describing the criteria to assess the activities of a member of the Public Council as follows:

The activities of the members of the Public Council are assessed according to the criteria for the effectiveness of work and the performance of their duties.

Each member of the Public Council regularly reports once every six months at meetings about his activities in the Public Council according to key indicators according to five criteria:

- Organisational indicator – the regularity of attendance of the meetings of the Public Council, participation in the activities of the Public Council,

- Work in the Commission – execution of commissions within the Commissions, organisation of hearings, etc.

- Work with government bodies – the number of requests to state bodies; the number of recommendations proposed and accepted for consideration by state bodies; Participation in the development of IPA, etc.

- Work with NGOs and citizens – the number of responses to citizens' appeals, essentially the treatment; work on the projects proposed by NGOs and citizens on the development of the city.

> - Openness and publicity – the amount of information and publications on the activities of the Public Council in the media, Internet resources, accessibility for the media, etc.
>
> Conducting this assessment led to some members withdrawing from the council, and revising the selection criteria for membership.
>
> The assessment procedure also brought valuable suggestions and recommendations by council members to strengthen the work of thematic commissions within the council.
>
> Source: response by Almaty Public Council, OECD survey in June 2018.

However, these indicators give information only on the process and not the effect that was sought or in effect achieved. The right type of indicators must be selected to evaluate the process, the immediate results, and also the indirect effect of practices on the governance culture.

Recommendations for setting indicators to measure the success of public councils

It is useful for policy makers to consider adopting a set of indicators to describe the effect of the public councils' work. Once the indicators have been decided upon, a system must be set up to collect the information, which will be regularly monitored.

The provisional indicators for monitoring the impact of public councils' work are proposed by the OECD as follows and are open for discussion:

Indicator 1: Is the community interested in council activities, and are citizens interacting with the council?

Monitoring the uptake of information channels and of specific topics published on websites or social media channels gives feedback on this indicator. The uptake can be measured by the counter on usage of the public channels and news items, to verify if the news item is shared on other social media sites, and picked up by media outlets.

Indicator 2: What share of proposals submitted by the council in the course of public consultations was addressed in official decisions, or adopted normative acts?

This indicator can be monitored by comparing the final version of decisions (official documents) to identify changes that correspond to comments and proposals suggested by the councils.

Indicator 3: Does the government practice improve in questions raised by councils (either by way of public monitoring or at public expertise).

The process of making actual changes in the public service and administrative standards can take time, so this indicator has to be monitored over a course of a longer time period. However, any changes can be traced if the council asks the authorities to proactively share information that is relevant to the initiative.

Conclusion

Stakeholder participation is increasingly recognised as an important mechanism to improve the quality of public policies and services, increase compliance with regulations, enhance transparency and build better interaction between citizens and public institutions.

New, innovative forms of participation are emerging all across the world, many of which include elements of citizen engagement such as co-creating policies and public services.

The principle challenge for countries, including OECD member countries, is to set up a governance culture and institutions to enable open government agenda to take root in practice. This requires building a shared vision and strategic roadmap not only within the public sector and all levels of government, but even more within society at large.

There are several positive effects of shifting towards an open governance approach for achieving inclusive growth.

To ensure positive outcomes that have been set forth in the national vision, the governance system in Kazakhstan needs to be open and demand-driven. Public institutions and their policies will need to become more accessible and more proactive in listening and integrating citizens' voices. This also implies the capacity to enable different levels of participation, from information to engagement. It foresees building new partnerships, and the capacity for government to move from "directing" to "steering", and to re-examine the "how" and "who" to include. This could be direct (citizens and businesses expressing their voice themselves) or indirect (through representative NGOs, business chambers, and public councils) (OECD, 2016b).

The methods for practical implementation of participation processes could involve information and communication technologies (ICTs) and on-line interfaces, or traditional face-to-face meetings, public hearings and regular public reporting.

The report described the present practices in the work of public councils in Kazakhstan according to their mandate set by the law. It identified the key elements for creating a solid foundation for stakeholder participation using regulatory, institutional and capacity building framework.

Throughout the guidance, the recommendations for improving public councils is supported by sharing practices in enabling stakeholder participation that can be found across the OECD countries and in different parts of the world.

This report also provides guidelines and recommendations that could inspire the improvement for public councils to become more transparent, more legitimate and more effective in serving the society in Kazakhstan.

Notes

[1] Ministry for Social Development, website accessed on May 12, 2018 at https://akk.diakom.gov.kz/ru/content/obshchestven. Note: public councils cannot be formed at the Supreme Court, the Constitutional Council, the prosecutor's office, the Presidential Administration, the National Bank, the Ministry of Defence, the Presidential Administration Office, the Prime Minister's Office, the Economic Department of the Parliament, the National Centre for Human Rights, the Accounts Committee for Control over the Execution of the Republican Budget, and the Central Election Commission.

[2] In August 2018, the Ministry for Social Development has drafted a proposal to amend the present Law on Public Councils, suggesting that 9/10 of their members should be Civil Society representatives.

[3] Ministry for Social Development analysis, website consulted in May 2018 at https://akk.diakom.gov.kz/ru/content/obshchestven

[4] Ministry for Social Development, draft recommendation on Internal working procedures, forthcoming.

[5] Ministry for Social Development website, accessed on May 20, 2018 at https://akk.diakom.gov.kz/ru/content/obshchestven

[6] Methodological guide for implementing public monitoring, Ministry for Social Development, website accessed on May 18, 2018 and revised version in August 2018 https://akk.diakom.gov.kz/ru/content/obshchestven

[7] In August 2018, the Ministry for Social Development has drafted a proposal to amend the present Law on Public Councils, suggesting that 9/10 of members should be Civil Society representatives.

[8] In the draft proposal to amend the Law on Public Councils, the Ministry for Social Development is proposing that each public institution compensate the costs for external expertise in reviewing draft legal acts and conducting public monitoring, if there is a budget available for these purposes.

References

Kazakhstan Citizens Alliance, report published on website of Ministry for Social Development) accessed on May 12, 2018 http://kazkenes.kz/articles/default/view?id=21

Law on Atameken, http://kazkenes.kz/laws

Law on Legal Acts, https://legalacts.egov.kz/

Law on Public Councils, as amended on July 11, 2017 http://kazkenes.kz/laws

Ministry of Religious Affairs and Civil Society, website accessed on May 12, 2018 at https://akk.diakom.gov.kz/ru/content/obshchestven.

Noor, K., Uus, M. (2011) in *Riigikogu toimetised*, publication series of the Parliament of Estonia, (in Estonian), https://rito.riigikogu.ee/eelmised-numbrid/nr-23/alalised-nouandvad-kogud-kaasamisvormina/

OECD (2017), Towards an Open Government in Kazakhstan, OECD Public Governance Reviews, OECD Publishing, Paris.

OECD (2016), The Governance of Inclusive Growth: An Overview of Country Initiatives, OECD Publishing, Paris .

OECD (2014), Regulatory Policy in Kazakhstan: Towards Improved Implementation, OECD Publishing, Paris. http://dx.doi.org/10.1787/9789264214255-en

OECD (2012) OECD Council Recommendation on Regulation Policy and Governance www.oecd.org/regreform/regulatory-policy/2012recommendation.htm

OECD (2003), Open Government: Fostering Dialogue with Civil Society. OECD Publishing, Paris.

Prager K. (2016), *Is co-creation more than participation?* in Integration and Implementation Insights, https://i2insights.org/2016/07/28/co-creation-or-participation/

State of the Nation Address by President of Kazakhstan Nursultan Nazarbayev. November 30, 2015, http://www.akorda.kz/en/addresses/state-of-the-nation-address-by-president-of-kazakhstan-nursultan-nazarbayev-november-30-2015

www.ingramcontent.com/pod-product-compliance
Lightning Source LLC
Chambersburg PA
CBHW081422270326
41931CB00015B/3377